THE SEMICONDUCTING
DICTIONARY

(Our Strindberg)

THE SEMICONDUCTING DICTIONARY

(Our Strindberg)

NATALEE CAPLE

MISFIT

ECW Press

Published by ECW Press
2120 Queen Street East, Suite 200, Toronto, Ontario, Canada M4E 1E2
416-694-3348 / info@ecwpress.com

LIBRARY AND ARCHIVES CANADA CATALOGUING IN PUBLICATION

Caple, Natalee, 1970-
The semiconducting dictionary : our Strindberg / Natalee Caple.

Poems.
ISBN 978-1-55022-982-0

1. Strindberg, August, 1849-1912—Poetry. I. Title.

PS8555.A5583S46 2010   C811'.54   C2010-901257-7

Editor for the press: Michael Holmes / a misFit book
Typesetting: Gail Nina
Cover design: Dave Gee
Text design: Tania Craan
Printing: Coach House Printing 1 2 3 4 5

The publication of *The Semiconducting Dictionary: Our Strindberg* has been generously
supported by the Canada Council for the Arts which last year invested $20.1 million in
writing and publishing throughout Canada, by the Ontario Arts Council, by the Government
of Ontario through Ontario Book Publishing Tax Credit, by the OMDC Book Fund, an
initiative of the Ontario Media Development Corporation, and by the Government of
Canada through the Canada Book Fund.

 Canada Council Conseil des Arts  Canadä ONTARIO ARTS COUNCIL
for the Arts   du Canada   CONSEIL DES ARTS DE L'ONTARIO

PRINTED AND BOUND IN CANADA

ECW PRESS
ecwpress.com

CONTENTS

This book is for Jeremy and the two little souls who called us together (Cassius and Imogen).

"*I* is a place. You can live here."

See me in the embryo
Time still outside

Heart that hovers in a glass chest
Perfect alien knees

Moths between
Soft walls of influence

No sex or language
Cliff edge before daylight

22 January 1849	Born in Stockholm, the third child of a shipping merchant and his former servant.
1853	Father goes bankrupt.
1854	Mother dies.
1855	Father marries another servant.
1867	Begins to dress as a man.
1868	Goes to Uppsala University. Decides to become a doctor.
1869	Fails exams. Leaves Uppsala. Writes first plays, *A Name, The Only Freethinker*.
1870	Returns to Uppsala to learn languages.
1871	Fourth play, *When in Rome*, is performed briefly at the Royal Theatre in Stockholm.
1872	Leaves Uppsala and settles in Stockholm. Tries to go onstage as an actor and fails.
1873	Becomes a journalist.
1874	Becomes a librarian.
1877	Marries Finnish actress, Siri von Essen.
1878	Reveals her sex to von Essen.
1879	Establishes herself as an author with the autobiographical novel, *The Red Rumour*.
1880	Writes historical fiction. Also, *The New King*, a provocative novel for which she is venomously attacked.
1883	Leaves Sweden. Travels abroad to France, Switzerland, Germany, and Denmark. First theatrical success with *Lucky Little Journey*.
1884	Publishes volume of short stories, *Marriage*. Is prosecuted for blasphemy but acquitted.
1885	Writes a novel about childhood, *The Servant's Girl*.

1886	Writes *The Stupid Father* in Bavaria. Writes *Madness: My Defense*, an account of marriage to von Essen.
1887	*The Stupid Father* is staged in Berlin. Becomes known across Germany. Writes *Miss Julie and the Creditors* in Denmark. *Miss Julie and the Creditors* is rawly attacked on publication for immorality.
1888	Starts experimental theatre in Denmark to stage own plays. Theatre goes bankrupt. Returns to Sweden and divorces von Essen.
1892	Visits England.
1893	*Miss Julie and the Creditors* staged in Paris. Is lionized but makes little money. Writes *A Lot of Nonsense* in French.
1894–1896	Destitute in Paris.
1896	Emerges from a mental crisis and returns to Sweden.
1897	Marries Harriet Bosse. Dabbles in alchemy. Returns to journalism. Hovers on the brink of insanity.
1898	Writes an effective account of insanity, the now forgotten *Inferno*.
1899	Divorces Harriet Bosse. Writes eleven plays.
1900	Tries again to make gold.
1901	Meets a Norwegian actress twenty-five years her junior. Writes fifteen plays.
1902	Left by the Norwegian actress who goes back to Norway. Writes no plays. Reputation in decline.
1909–1912	Writes chamber plays, which are coldly received.

1912–1915	Devotes last three years of life to writing pamphlets on politics and philosophy.
14 May 1915	Dies in Stockholm of uterine cancer, aged sixty-six. Attended at her death by a maidservant.

Christmas Poem by My Mother

It's Christmas
And we need each other
One tree is on the low sky
I have seen that tree before
Dreams across the hills collect
Like silver knives in a velvet pouch
An alien who landed here might say
How busy we are how little time
We have for each other
Feelings teem beneath chaste berries
So glad to see cold breath fall from loved ones' lips
How awkward and how perfect the city
The ice-skaters and the lights
If I didn't tell you before let me tell you now
I love you Merry Christmas

Smash the Poem

Flung is radiate heat comes sew whispers breathes is screwed
carried sleeping smoking memorize seems read is can't be lost
burn try sits turns cries is

Sheets windows light family enemies peace floors woman suits
she corner she word faith coffin hall room brothers funeral
summer leisure names plants nothing knowledge capitol sheets
everything acid attic battery copper zinc time sock child herself
stillness rooms

White soft now enough new asleep such extraordinary shut
through long strange lost sulphuric old Daniellian inward dry

Over the all the to the a to in the that with the and the in a with
after the the of the of until because a that be the with in the a of
like a after the there in the

,

White sheets flung windows light soft now family enemies
radiate peace enough heat floors woman comes sew new suits
she whispers corner asleep she breathes word such extraordinary
faith coffin screwed shut carried through hall sleeping room
brothers smoking funeral long summer leisure memorize names
plants nothing seems strange read knowledge capitol lost burn
sheets try everything sulphuric acid attic sits battery old
Daniellian copper zinc time turns inward sock child cries herself
dry stillness rooms

White sheets flung over the windows all the light is soft now
Family enemies radiate peace enough to heat the floors
A woman comes to sew new suits she whispers in the corner

Asleep, she breathes that word with such extraordinary faith
The coffin is screwed shut and carried through the hall
Sleeping in a room with brothers smoking
After the funeral the long summer of leisure
Memorize the names of plants until nothing seems strange
Read because knowledge is a capitol that can't be lost
Burn the sheets try everything with sulphuric acid
In the attic sits a battery of old Daniellian copper zinc
Time turns inward like a sock
After the child cries herself dry there is stillness in the rooms

Be a Child then and I Can Kiss It Better . . .

After all it is only a house
Cellar under the library where you hide to avoid friends

Thunder breaks the walls
Creditors eat the chairs

You paint the air with pollen

Leave the zombies in the opera house
Be the voice that shakes the century

Both drum and echoing chamber

Poem for My Mother

Secrets that my mother kept
Are not really poems
But the traces of her child-mind
The infant in the servant

M. I know you must die
But let us speak a little longer
Move our mouths
Around ideas in our hearts

At the end of each day
When I am sad
I conjure your loyal hands
Until I feel tender again

Franz Says

Every man carries a room about inside him
In the night the rattling of a mirror betrays the secret walls

Franz hates winter hates coal buckets hates the bloody whiteness
of the frozen plain of ice

I am far down in the silence
Dismounted following the tracks of dogs. There is no room
inside me

Discarded

Give up my card
Drain the wine and throw away the bottle
Sweep the rain from the stoop
Strangle the bird that does not sing
Devour the liver of an animal
Respect the devil in the Devil

Hesitate — a human moment

If I shall exist forever how will I know when forever begins?

Become a man. They have all the answers

The Servant's Girl: The Story of the Evolution of a Human Being '

Luther hid venereal disease craved marriage
Edison was too poor to travel
Lasalle the pig loved oysters
Iago hero of that play shrugs and says
I am nothing if not critical

Go ahead and be a vicious
Disobedient greedy bastard
For a thing said by a good man is not true

My mother knew a fixed heaven and a fixed hell
Saw a city upside down
Where the heaviest lie on the bottom
And the lightest float to the top
Poverty however democratic
Anchored by a low centre of gravity

Leave a dress in the grotto by Dido
Split my lip and shave my head
Rise and float by fatted angels
From the steps of a university
Leap and sever silken necks
Feast upon the declawed hands of aristocrats

In the space between villain and crime
In the cemetery under the sun
I cradle each discarded body
Until I can be a woman again

Recipe for Heart Troubles

Three ounces of gold dissolved in nitric acid
Three ounces of silver dissolved in nitric acid
Four ounces of common salt
Leave it all for twenty days
Distill into dryness
Dry salts represent the earth
Heat them until they give no fumes
Grind them in a glass vessel
To the finely divided gold and silver chloride
Add fixed salt from urine
Distill seven times
Warm over the gentle heat of ashes
Add one part mixture to three parts mercury
Add one part gold — now it is a paste
An "oil of gold"

Laura and the Captain

LAURA: Yes, that's how it was, I loved you.

CAPTAIN: I thought you despised my masculinity.

LAURA: I'm sleepy. Do you have any more fantasies?

CAPTAIN: I am riding a black horse and the world around me is black. My shoes and suit and the reins and bridle are all black. There is no sound to the universe. I can't smell anything.

LAURA: Are you dead?

CAPTAIN: Yes. You're such a clever thing.

LAURA: I have a fantasy too. A child has a wooden reel with a piece of string tied around it. It never occurs to him to pull the string along the floor and pretend it is attached to a pet. Instead, he throws the string over the edge of his cot so that it disappears, at the same time he utters "Oo-oo-ooo!" Then he reels the string in again and cries out with joy. That's the whole game, disappearance and reappearance, renunciation and retrieval.

CAPTAIN: Lay your little head here, on my chest. You feel so warm.

LAURA: I'm so sleepy. Does everyone babble when they are falling asleep?

CAPTAIN: No. I don't think businessmen or doctors babble. It's only foolish people who have been drinking wine and falling in love.

LAURA: When we first met I hated you.

CAPTAIN: That's all right. That's how it is with men and women, always hating and loving and loving and hating. It would be better if there were a third sex to mediate.

LAURA: A third sex?

CAPTAIN: Yes, something like a mother-in-law who can't speak, can only write on a chalkboard what we really mean when we can't remember ourselves.

A Country Road. A Tree. Evening.

Here the madman falls silent and looks again at his listeners.

QUESTION: What if, after all, the churches are the tombs and sepulchres of God? What if you discovered that your mystical explanations were not deep at all but in fact the most superficial? What if it took until dark to recognize the twilight of your idols?

ANSWER: I know that God lives. He makes a noise in me like feathers, like leaves. Like a long silence that makes me want to reach out to you. I must believe there is a soul and it is the conch shell in which those noises rest. My soul is the part of me that wants to live in spite of hunger, pain, or any monster in my cells. A flower heliotropes and I turn to the blood that directs my cheeks to blush. I know God lives because I cry and feel despair. What am I doing here with all the tigers and the snowstorms?

Notes for a New Play

POSSIBLE CHARACTER 1: Isn't it strange that her "authoring" fell off after the first book. But that first time the subject wrote itself. She used her former husband for a model. They say he was an idiot.

POSSIBLE CHARACTER 2: How soft the oats are, lying down in the oat bin. So like human skin. I shut the lid and close my eyes. I sink my limbs and give up hope of winning.

> *Wax candles gutter at the stage edge. A violin signals the distance. Dust in the theatre is illuminated by the open window. Can we paint the dust?*

> *Miss Julie moves the servant's body. She turns her back on the audience.*

MISS JULIE: And you have never wanted to be free?

SERVANT: Perhaps, when we get to the bottom of it that is just what has happened.

> *I think we need a parrot and some skeletons.*

Characters

CAPTAIN, in the cavalry
LAURA, his wife
BERTHA, their daughter, about fourteen years old
DR. EASTLAND
PASTOR, Protestant, Laura's brother Jonas
MARGARET, the Captain's old nurse
HAPPY, a corporal in the army
ORDERLY, the Captain's
AUTHOR, me

> *We begin. Action takes place in Sweden. It is December in the 1880s.*

The Stupid Father

The Captain's parlour a door to the rear
Another entrance a large round table
Sheaves of letters the wallpapered door red
Element glowing curtains drawn
Mere ticking weapons and the hour
Elapsing the clocks ticking the pendulum swinging
A gunbag by lamplight
Wild when the pastor arrives

Ah he rises yes sir yes sir are you happy here
Son of a gun has been
Too familiar the maid is pregnant
Little devil the cavalry's coming
Keep bawling him out now and thrash out his innards
God's every word as good as the drink on the table

My right eye if you're happy then tell the whole
Evil story about dancing with Gabriel
And singing a sermon
We're wasting time baby if you don't
Who acts now you told Emma something
To marry you promptly don't get the idea that
Two well-known painters will close the case with
A portrait of Bertha do I act nervous

Kill me I'm dying what did she tell you
Either the foot's in the grave sir man against
Mother some vile reason for sharing or
Ever returning her fault for being
A mother has no rights
We'll have to invent some
But it's in a law book

People have no sense and he's been your daddy
No he's been unfaithful there is so much illness
He needs to see planets revolving on slides and here is an
Other but we need a doctor so sorry
We only have pastors and maids

We Don't Speak of Eternal Love

Two actors and I create a world
With three I set it in motion
We don't speak of eternal love
Tableau of knees resting upon the sweet Madonna
That tables are hyphens between speakers
But settle our roles upon the mood from the wings
Become lionesses arriving at Easter
Enter as if revived by this world
In wonder and terror unite with the scene
Stress the effect of poisonous flowers
Driving him mad just like his father
Once every word becomes a knife
Try gently to coax her back to life

Origin of Species

I

The audience
Victorians in the swamp
Keening for more mud

II

Foreground a river
Church door shallow boat moored there
They pause by the tree

III

The whole subject of the theatre must, I think, remain vague; nevertheless, I may state that I think it highly probable that our actors (those domestic dogs) have descended from several wild species, including the madman, the preacher, and the drunk. In regard to setmakers and costumers I can form no opinion. I should think, from facts communicated to me by Mr. Blyth, that these had descended from a different aboriginal stock than our European carpenters and seamstresses; and several competent judges believe that these latter have had more than one wild parent. With respect to playwrights, for reasons I cannot give here, I am doubtfully inclined to believe, in opposition to several authors, that all the plays have descended from the one origin be it text or muse. Mr. Blyth, whose opinion, from his large and varied stores of knowledge, I should value more than that of almost anyone, thinks that all the movements of art have proceeded from variations on public seductions performed during weddings. In regard to dancers and clowns, the breeds of which differ considerably from each other in structure, I do not doubt that they all have descended from the common street urchin.

Taken for homeless
Beggar begins to divine
Her full beggar-ness

IV

I should premise that I use the phrase "Struggle for Existence" in a large and metaphorical sense, including the dependence of one art form upon another, and including (which is more important) not only the life of the individual, but success in establishing an oeuvre. Two canine animals in a time of dearth may be truly said to struggle with each other to get food and live. But a writer on the edge of the desert facing no reviews or readers is said to struggle for life against the drought, though more properly he should be said to be dependent on the popular culture (which does drip). A painter who annually produces fifty canvasses, of which on average only one sells, may be more truly said to struggle with other painters and paintings of the same and other kinds, which already clothe the walls of the wealthy. The sculptor is dependent on the quarry and a few other things like trees to build scaffolding, but can only in a far-fetched sense be said to struggle with trees. For, if too many sculptors scavenge from the same quarry or forest, it is not the rocks or the trees that will languish before they die. Several sculptors, working closely together on the same project, may most truly be said to struggle with each other. As the sculpture is hacked away by jealous hands, its existence depends upon the ability of one or all to stand back and allow fame to be dispersed among them; the sculpture then may metaphorically be said to struggle with other more practical stone products, such as bridges or tunnels or houses or fountains (which do more to tempt birds). In these several senses, which pass into each other, I use for convenience sake the general phrase "Struggle for Existence."

A struggle for existence inevitably follows from the high rate at which all organic beings tend to increase. In many cities there are, at present, too many poets (whom Nietzsche calls liars) and too few trees. Every being, which during its natural lifetime produces several books or works, must suffer deconstruction during some period of its life. And, during some season or occasional year on the principle of economic boom or recession, the numbers of competitors will seem quickly to become so inordinately great that no country can support them all. Hence, as more individuals are produced from art schools than can possibly survive, there must in every case be a struggle, either between one individual and another in the same genre, or between the individuals of a distinct movement, or between the physical conditions of life and all artists. It is the doctrine of Malthus applied with manifold force to the whole animal and vegetable kingdoms, and applied with especial force against the cultural worker; for in this case there can be no artificial increase of interest in poetry, and no prudential restraint from expenses on fashion, jewellery, or travel. Although some species of readers and patrons may be now increasing, more or less rapidly, in numbers, all cannot do so, for the world would not hold them.

She raises her head
A Catholic Requiem
Beggar sings loudly

V

Slave-making instinct. This remarkable instinct was first
discovered in the Formica (Polyamorous) refusents by Pierre
Huber, a better observer even than his celebrated father. This
community is absolutely dependent on its slaves; without their
aid, the whole society would certainly become extinct in a single
year. The males and fertile females do no work. The workers or
sterile females, though most energetic and courageous in
capturing slaves, do no other work. They are incapable of making
their own beds, or of feeding their own infants. When the old
towns and villages are found inconvenient, and they have to
immigrate, it is the slaves who determine the course of the
immigration, and actually carry their masters. So utterly helpless
are the masters, that when Huber shut up thirty of them without
a slave, but with plenty of the food which they liked best, and
with their infants and pets to stimulate them to work, they did
nothing; they could not even feed themselves, and many perished
of hunger. Huber then introduced a single slave and she instantly
set to work, fed and saved the survivors, made some cells and
tended the young ones, and put all to rights. What can be more
extraordinary than these well-ascertained facts? What can be a
greater evidence of the reliance of all society upon the existence
of a servant class? If we had not known of any other slave-
making people, it would have been hopeless to have speculated
how so wonderful an instinct could have been perfected.

Enter the servants
Dancing in country-style frocks
Miss Julie stage left

VI

The view generally entertained by naturalists is that the genders, when not intercrossed, have been specially endowed with the quality of sterility, in order to prevent the confusion of all organic forms. This view certainly seems at first probable, for men and women within the same country could hardly have kept distinct had they been capable of crossing freely and creating more genders. Who after all, would choose to be a woman if there were options other than to be a man? The importance of the fact that hybrids of all types are very generally sterile, has, I think, been much underrated. However, on the theory of natural selection the case is especially important, inasmuch as the sterility of male-male or female-female relations, because the progeny of such couplings (if they could happen) would hold special advantage over the progeny of male-female couplings because of their intrinsic genetic creativity and the sudden imperative to lift limits on both genders once their boundaries had been breached (it has been already remarked, that the degree of fertility, both of first crosses and of hybrids, graduates from zero to perfect fertility). The old binaries would become instantly suffocating and antiquated, until, after some time, the performance of being either a man or a woman would become part of a fashion, as is the course of all old machinery and textiles. To employ or wear a gender would seem at first to be behind the times, then to be retrospective, and finally to be futuristic. The threat of such an interpretation would create countercultures and localized denial in the form of arguments for the continued preservation of successive profitable degrees of sterility. I hope, however, to be able to show that fertility or sterility are neither specially acquired nor endowed qualities, but are, in fact, incidental to other acquired differences that accomplish the same goals. Also, I hope that since the "woman question" cannot be answered until women can answer and it is clear that nobody wants that, I can present another option in the utter assimilation of both genders by one another.

Jean says to Julie
There are barriers between us
Watch me climb to you

Eavesdropping

They say I lie
I am lost with
Sheets and branches to the sea
Sky grace door peace discomfort harm
Whiswhiswhis ha ha k'ough
Smelling smoke the something burning is a part of me
I am not a mirror for when he left
I was embarrassed to want things
A bird hit by two stones
Tongue tries and dries
Vessel of some fool breaking into banks of air
Wholesale of songs sung loud against machines
Stumble stumble stammer stammer
She disappears into the station
Raise your heads out of the cold and stare

Poem from the Play

If you must be then say
We live in legions
We think or feel or maybe I don't know if we do
Who is thinking this place and where is it
Where are the souls that multiply if
I I I I exist
In your indifferent silent hands
I speak in thrusts of I feel or I think or I don't
Crisscross I I but you
Dictate to the unknown
Trusting hurts the
I to whom I write

Cheerful Books Believe

Pound clothes upon the stones
        Sing!   Sing!

Alive! Alive!

        Ha!   Ha!

                                I am an animal
                                I am an animal
                                I am an animal

                            And it makes me happy
                                    to see you

The Playwright Interviews Herself to Stave Off Loneliness

What is the main trait to your character?
It must be melancholy.

What do you prize most highly in a man?
His narrow-mindedness. His dreams in which he is always at the
centre of an ice storm.

What do you prize most highly in a woman?
Her weakness. Her loving heart. Her ability to keep things clean.

Which talent would you most like to possess?
The ability to travel forward in time.

Which fault would you like least to possess?
Narrow-mindedness. Melancholy.

What is your favourite occupation?
To write plays.

What is the greatest happiness you can imagine?
Siri and me in our warm skins on the sand.

What do you want?
To be a famous playwright whose plays run day and night
everywhere in every language.

What is the greatest misfortune you can imagine?
To be without Siri and unable to write. To be unable to write.

Where would you like to live?
In the Stockholm skerries.

What is your favourite colour?
Zinc yellow. Amethyst violet.

What is your favourite flower?
Cyclamen.

What is your favourite creature?
The blue butterfly.

Which books do you admire most?
Hans Christian Andersen's Fairy Tales. The Bible, for its ending.

Which painting do you admire most?
Théodore Rousseau's paysages intimes. Everything by Turner.

Which music do you love most?
Beethoven's Sonatas.

Which fictional male characters attract you most?
Louis Lambert, Balzac; the Bishop in *Les Misérables*, Hugo.

Which fictitious female character attracts you most?
Margaretha in *Faust*.

What is your favourite name?
Margaretha.

Which human fault is the easiest to forgive?
Extravagance.

Which season do you like the best?
Height of summer in the warm rain.

What are your favourite drinks and dishes?
Beer and fish.

What is your motto?
Speravit infestis.

Life in One Act

Waters blue plants pink evening sweetens girl dresses palace
opens painters work curtains rustle program begins actors bow
(and now they drink) wine decants dandy laughs music falls taxis
pause horses breathe fog settles hotel brims hand fumbles key
turns room unfolds bed welcomes pillow dreams day recedes
eyelids flicker mouth snores stomach grumbles legs twitch arms
reach cheek creases hair musses lips buss bum itches hand
scratches tongue swallows throat sighs tears gather light enters
birds twitter traffic bustles sun rises merchants call windows
reflect church bell tolls world revolves angels dicker fish swim
weavers weave sculptors saw nurses bathe babies mew chopsticks
click potatoes stew passage opens columns stand roofs slant walls
hold fireplace glows tea brews dough rises grain leans cows chew
clouds creep rain gathers lake swells waters blue

To Have Done With the Judgment of Dogs

There are those who wish to boo. But this booing is not well founded. Photograph the grain of dust on the camera lens; this is realism. Zola *elevates* the murder of a spouse — its natural freshness sifts through the censor's sieve. Nature delights in the struggle between the forest and the tree, the deep desire to claim space but the censor, who is so dull that after four hours of suffering he still seeks naturalism in a piece of Nature, sees the point where battles are fought, rebellion and instinct, as stages for grandiose art. Action, if it can be called action, happens when the old woman lies in bed dying; beside her stand three sons. She makes a sign — one son was conceived in adultery. Lamentation around the deathbed is actually for the sunny morning. There are days when I despise myself for nothing touches me anymore.

Too Much

Tell me the truth
The big joke of the day
We love what is great in Nature
Because in our heads we are great

Listen again with eyes closed
Trees move in the forest
What is closest appears large
That is the law of Egoism

Siri

I sat at the edge of a little stream
Thinking of drowning myself
She ran along the high road
The soles of her feet lifted

I wore a pair of suspenders
Thinking of following her
She ran along the high road
Her calves and thighs bare

I was like her under my suspenders
Thinking of grabbing her waist
She ran along the high road
Her arms pumped the air

I touched myself harshly by the little stream
She ran along the high road
Cheeks and lips bright red

Perfect Early Days

Look at the white orchid beside its red sister
As if the fields remember only weddings
Come climb with me the forests wait
Hike up your sleeves and skirt
Tie your curls behind your neck
We are equals in the sunshine laughing
Tonight we'll name the stars for pets

Darling Siri Writes a Christmas Poem by Pretending to Read French

La tzigane savait d'avance
Nos deux vies barrées par les nuits
Nous lui dîmes adieu et puis
De ce puits sortit l'Espérance

L'amour lourd comme un ours privé
Dansa debout quand nous voulûmes
Et l'oiseau bleu perdit ses plumes
Et les mendiants leurs Ave

On sait très bien que l'on se damne
Mais l'espoir d'aimer en chemin
Nous fait penser main dans la main
À ce qu'an prédit la tzigane

The gypsy knew in advance
To tip up the barrels and spill out the night
He slipped coins through the lips of the poor with a kiss
This, he thought, is a starry map to hope

He danced alone at night like a gleeful bear
He wore his secret love like a furry sweater
His cousin predicted a novel in his future
He made the merchants soften and dole out sweets

This is the way that the world should be
Love and sweaters the norm
Let's pretend we are holding hands
And we can be gypsies all year

Precious Arrival

The child is the little soul that calls
Two people together because it wants to make parents of them
The atomic little one so hot in the mornings
Calm and threatening days washed out with celery kisses
My life shrinks around me
O you who never hates me
And she the lovely tourmaline
Set deep in the rudder of our bedroom

For You

My shoes are filled with amarynth
My wallet filled with wine
My mouth is full of ladybugs
My panties filled with thyme
I broke my arm on a daffodil
You broke yours there too
And now we get a holiday
In lovely gay Peru

Happy Animal

Green birds love tinsel
And red birds love silk
Gold birds love liquor
And blue birds love milk

Lizards love butter
And camels love steak
Night owls love windmills
And foxes love cake

The world loves the moonbeams
The moon loves the sky
The sky loves the ocean
No one knows why

Letter from Paris, 1883

Dear Siri,

I am poor and alone in Paris. I miss your lovely skin. Against my usual habits I have read my book in print. I find it seminal. It is like an honest and good copulation compared with Ibsen's hysterical jerking off. And there was a damned lot of fucking among the haycocks.

In Paris, all the beauty annoys me and there are too many good smells. I am beginning to think that it is my nature that I don't really want to be happy. But then today over coffee I found out something horrible that someone did to someone else. Even though I am not involved, I feel a little sick to be reminded of the things that people do to each other. And I realize that I do not like that feeling.

I cannot use names but say a man has a wife, and say he does not love her. Say this man was once a famous writer but for thirty years he has been nobody. Still, even I can see there is some shimmer of his former self around his face and women feel such ridiculous optimism. I know how love between men and women can vacillate from adoration to contempt. But this is different, Siri. So, she loves him. You know him and there is nothing much to love but what there is she magnifies. Then comes all the bad news, the marriage caked in infidelity, the drinking, and the insults, but that's all ordinary. This woman, a lovely woman with red hair and a loud, crunchy voice, knows everything about this man, every unspeakable thing that we turn our faces from. It breaks her heart that she still loves him.

And this man, he is utterly lacking in everything, a terrible waste of oxygen. But respectable still, for everyone likes his wife. He takes her money. He tells her to cover up her aging breasts. He leaves with another woman. He sells all their wedding gifts. He reads her love letters to his mistress. He tells her if she cannot bear it she should go ahead, feel free to die. He brings his mistress to her funeral.

That night he walks the streets, strolls through the Tuileries, and then beside the Louvre. A weight lifts from his narrow batwing shoulders. She, at last, is gone. Her stupid love is gone. At the corner he enters a bar and sits, watches as the fat barman draws the ale. You look sad, a pretty girl tells him. Turning on his stool, he croons, my beautiful wife is dead.

And what are we to do with this, my sweet and innocent girl? There is no way to humiliate a creature that has no shame. I will see him at the concert next week. I should scream, *How dare you? How dare you* treat another person that way? I should throw darts at his smug, poisonous grin, break his hideous teeth. I should let out the rageful bird inside me. But I know about myself that I have no appetite for revenge, not for myself or for humanity. My desire for peace unsettles me. The band will start up. I will take my seat and flip through the program. He will sit across from me with the musicians between us. The only thing I can imagine is that I will invent some killing look to give every time I meet his eyes, which says, I see you. I hate you. I know. I *see* you. I *hate* you. I *know*. Nietzsche says that you cannot judge a man by how he treats another man but by how he treats his woman or his horse. I don't like the comparison but I see his point. Cruelty is all about letting out the darkness when you feel invisible.

Siri, I will be missing you. Every night when I am sad I kiss your little picture. I have no wish at all to be a "great" writer, let alone a great man. It would just embarrass me and betray a false position. I want to go in nightgown and underwear and be known as a scandal-writer, that wouldn't embarrass me. But looking at this man does embarrass me. I promise I will learn from his actions and try every day to keep becoming kinder. Promise me that if I don't, or if I can't, you will do the right thing and kill me instead of your dear self.

I love you. I love you.

Your *August S.*

Sunday in Stockholm

On Sunday I blaze by cobbled streets
Kiss the washerwoman thoughts all happy
Full of birds whose lives unfold half in the skies
The torrents of fish that rage beneath
Shaken waves at daybreak

At dusk I streak outside my haunts
Beer glasses scrubbed beside whiskey bottles
Telling tales of lazy-love
To foolish friends who lean against the night
Mocked by tethered horses

Asleep I dream of women
Hanging on the bones of windowsills
In the rusty-shuttered night
Shame of flesh see-sawing over blind farmhands
Fewer loves between them than the dust

Wake to watch the stars fall
Chide myself I hear the talking salmon
Women turn to girls sleeping under blankets
In blond hotel rooms by the skerries
Counting nanny goats until the morning

J. W. Turner's Will

To the decaying artists I leave one thousand
Watercolours and drawings
Dido rain steam speed
Haircuts from my father little map of London
Coins from Venice all my cash
You do not need to hide like me
In a little house before you die I
Will not line my casket with
Things I cannot see

Fifteen a painting hung
In the Royal Academy eighteen
Playing in my own studio twenty
And the printers copy all my strokes
I did not paint the sea I painted
What the sea painted in me
Thirty I become eccentric
(That is what they call you
When your father is your best friend)

But remember I was rich
And him and me we lost her
Before my memory set in
So when I paint in black rain
Or red forces burning houses of lords
Even in the grand canals
I paint a window to that death
A drop of pigment might be her
Why should I sell the rest?

Revolution

Why were there more people
When the trains began to run
Shipping peasants to the cities
Shuffling unsure

Farms spilled pumpkins lumpers corn
We ate and ate
Aristocrats spun rings on fingers
More brown eyes they thought more black hair

India surrendered cotton tea and dizzy patterns
We needed more clothes
Because we were fat
Fly-shuttle and spinning jenny

England nested on beds of coal
Until she tore the nest apart
Replaced the wood of ancient fires
With dinosaurs and bones of leaves

Steel was the new province
Mined until the deeper holes filled with water
Then built beasts to run on steam
Single piston engines

Circling eyeing Europe
Fogging up the borders
At the end of absolutism
As the Enlightenment waned

Escape

Escape the sweated trades
A little polish on your cheek

Lungs expel prayer
Arteries of train tracks spreading

Addiction to the giddy atlas
At last the sheets of rock and valleys

Open onto Polish mountains
A Carpathian passage green

Action Always Action

Madame fingers the ivory keyboard
Thinking of Bluebeard, dreaming his brain
As soon as the idea subsides
Flower bells tip out the rain

Siri begs me to stop thinking.
Come on — I say — come on!

Children relish playing Papa
Whipping each other with sticks
Crying makes the hours pass
Evening hours already swollen

But her little nipples make me laugh
I kiss her musical mouth
As if a hundred nameless girls desire
Flush to the furthermost terrain

M

My cat who looks at me in the bathroom
My cat who does not answer strangers
My cat whose fur is the antidote for strong pain
My cat named for Africa
My cat with tiny paws dipped in clear anise
My cat by moonlight in a snowstorm
My cat with empty legs that beat the air
My cat screaming in my arms
My cat who nibbles on my drunken earlobes
My cat laying flat in sunspots
My cat lapping at the capsized cup
My cat at work upon her first novel
My cat trembling in the grove of orange trees
My cat travelling to France
My cat beginning again in a cold town
My cat afraid of shadows and the light that casts them
My cat knowing people seeing all their weakness
My cat done wrong by
My cat who is real and not some prosaic metaphor
My cat knowing books and how it is to doze upon their spines
My cat boxing the dawn
My cat a harbinger of how the world could be
My cat who forgives completely
My cat blacker than time after death
My cat in the forest-fire of recollection
My cat fantastic before the flood
My cat upon a leaky ark calling to her kittens
My cat dreamt of by a songwriter
My cat who beheads seditious mice
My cat who believes in angels
My cat *qui embrasse mes paupières mouillées*

Modern Sins

The sin of electricity is the failure of the night to resist the day
Myths of matrimony a sound like footsteps round the bed
Words lying dreamless across a warm belly

A new master a new slave a new mouth a new hole a new day a
new thought a new shape a new bruise a new taste a new sheet a
new word meaning something new anew

Look Back

No light shows through your skin, tender heart agape. As if you opened a book and saw there the terrible things that would happen to the one you loved the most and when you dropped the book and ran to the door you found it locked.

Insults

See the dead sky
Tell me, Siri, do you
Wonder why the playwright ignores you
Why his stare
Depresses you

He is worried by your aging skin
That each day
Recommends a new life
He knows you plot against him
Planting the smell of burning toast

Everything under the big dead sky
Asks why do you even bother
You charm only the lilies

Your Attention PLEASE *[A Poem by Once-Darling Siri]*

May I remind you
That your slippered feet do not tread alone
The Persian carpet or the soft brown dirt
By your ear a feathery hum a honey sound
A heart too small to stop
Why ignore the Carnival of Senses?
Sibilant beneath the clouds
The clouds! The day breaks over brown rooftops
A white trumpet flower
In the pale pink palm of my hand
My silly mouth
Filled with cold water
And the squeaky dolphins
Incessantly urging you home

Darling Troublemaker *[Siri]*

You say you are alone in the world
Brilliant when I look at you

The breath that billows from your lips turns the stars to violets
I keep trying to speak but the words they have no sound

It isn't that you must be humble or that I think you're vain or
cruel or desperately detached

Darling Troublemaker there is no problem to be solved
I still believe that faith answers the questions of labouring souls

When we come back to the ocean we all come apart
Flow through the mouths of sea turtles like the salted waves

Swaying back and forth

Please *[Siri]*

Speak to me more softly
Batter away the insignificant stuttering of your first thought
O what vows I heard you make to the sea
                   when you bent your head to the red starfish

Ours *[Siri]*

What makes me forgive you
It must be the way

I think you are still away from me

Dream the great wide head of a black bear
Leans down to look at me in bed

Claws sheathe into my hair

I hear your voice whisper
"I wanted so not to hurt you"

Quiet August *[One Last Try by Siri]*

Between the shadow of your hand and your hand
the air barely moves
I am afraid like you that we do not exist
There are too many seconds too many doubts
Your work is your baby your cathedral
I do try to cry quietly
That night the night your modern friends decided that nothing
matters and the end of the world was arriving I wanted the sky
to collapse like a silk parachute over our skinned bodies
Be forgiven in softness I wanted to be religious again
Understood by the light behind the door
I wanted to alter the registration of time
and draw you from that emptiness
I wanted to fall asleep unaware
A filament filled with light, stubborn love

She Leaves Me

At the edge of departure I see
Your lovely fingernails as you study them
My winter-saturated hair
The trolley tracks blurring

The little one at breakfast
In her coat and shoes
Why didn't we plant the garden
With cucumbers and strawberries?

Why did we argue over God?
The bedsheets still need washing
My words curve around you
You are an island with an engine

I write to ambush roses cut them up
I do not understand your gifts
And now the ticket and the suitcase
Move away from me with faint touch

Illustrations

Declaration

And the theatre could be perfect if the streets could lead to the
ocean if the gallery could be made of glass if the mailbox could
be full of money if the deaths could be poetic if the Arc de
Triomphe could be an island if the twilight could be damp if the
boundary stone could be toffee if the victory could be a relief if
the Seine could be flooded if the gates could fly open if the
vaults could be emptied if the water could be wine if the vistas
could prove their existence if the moment could pass without
taxes if the bucket could walk after filling if the steamboat could
run on illusions if the newspaper could sing all the sad parts if
the discourse could break in the middle if the dream could
become a sculpture if the day could be everlasting if the
entwinkling stars could fall if the follies of all were forgiven if
the cholera could call an ambulance if the uniforms could be
made of rubber if the barricades could hold the infantry if the
fountains could vote for the roses if the horses could write to
the emperor if the artists could all be paid if the weddings could
happen in France if the colours could sleep by the easel if

Dear Siri

For hurting me for giving up on me for failing to understand my genius for removing your love from me for wanting something outside of me for removing our child from me for refusing to give me any more money for questioning me for criticizing me for falling in love with someone else every step you take in a direction away from me you will feel pain shoot up your legs and arms. You will be able to measure the distance between us by the degree of your pain. I will live as if you do not exist for indeed you have forfeited that right. I will forget you completely and I will encourage others to do so as well. I will spread rumours that you are a lesbian and you took all my money. I will turn your friends against you. I will surround you with silence. I will serve champagne to everyone but you. I will erase you. I will erase you. Come back to me or suffer.

Dear Friend Ibsen

I despise you. By reading this letter you activate my powers. These words are maggots unfurling in your brain. From now on you will hang my picture on your wall. You will be unable to write except under my gaze. Your plays, which were never very good, will become more and more execrable. This is the code that you must break in order to be free of me 4444-444!

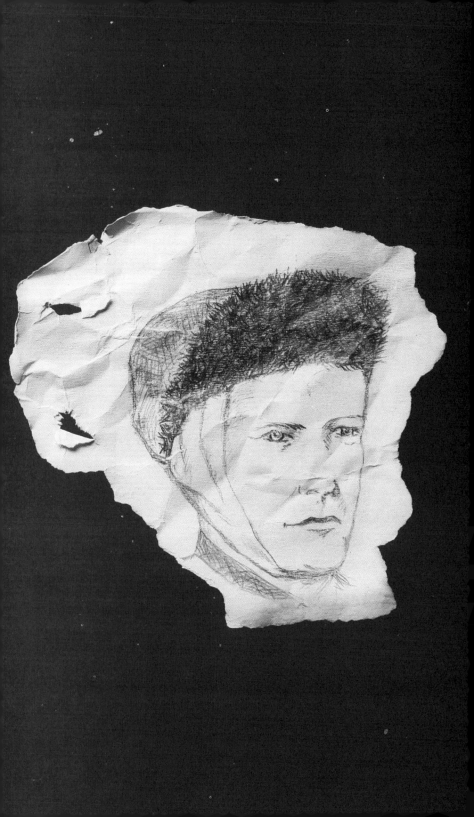

Darling Daughter

Pin this spell near your heart. Whenever you need me close your eyes and I will see you. This spell will protect you from any kind of harm. Understand there will be no harm that can touch you. Touch the spell when you are in danger and whoever or whatever poses the danger to you will explode. Touch this spell when you are sick and you will be well again. This spell is my heart and all of its contents. This spell is more powerful than money. I give it to you because you are more valuable than fame. You are more rare than talent. You are my only friend.

Dear Siri

This spell cancels the other spell I sent you. This spell makes you forgive me.

Dear Future

When you read this it will become clear that the upper classes
were dependent upon the lower classes and that gender was itself
a class. The audience and not the actors were puppets, being
moved to tears by a text that knew nothing of them. It will
become clear that I was wronged by time by Bohemians who
only count lint by the saddlemaker who arranged the thing to
bruise me by the doctors who exposed me and the prostitute
who laughed by my body by my brothers by my little dog and
the critics and Ibsen and every idiot in the theatre by the
politicians who had me for dinner by debates held about my
value. I was wronged because I had no vote. I loved my child. I
loved my wife. I loved my family, even my father, Oskar. I cared
about the theatre and I treasured the actresses. I adored all the
cities but most of all Stockholm. I ate flowers for breakfast until I
was nine. I tutored wealthy children and they loved me. I could
paint. I could be kind. I was at times the finest of beings. I was at
times a perfect mirror of humankind.

She speaks now as if
You could hear a woman's speech
Cricket-song heartbeat

Dear Reader

Because this book is haunted (although perhaps no more than any other) when you read this I will be. Thank you. You need not have any company or read me well or even enjoy me. If you remember that you read this book it is enough. Because you read a new me is here and she retains a trace of someone who lost every battle. I was a girl a student a librarian an actor a journalist a husband a father a writer a painter an alchemist a madman and a poet. I tried hard at all these things but it did not go well. Still, there was immeasurable value to my life. Please know that I appreciate the cells in which I now dwell. I sit here with a funny sort of crowd. We cheer for you. There is magic in you.

Beloved Reader
After my demise I hope
The sweet world will thrive

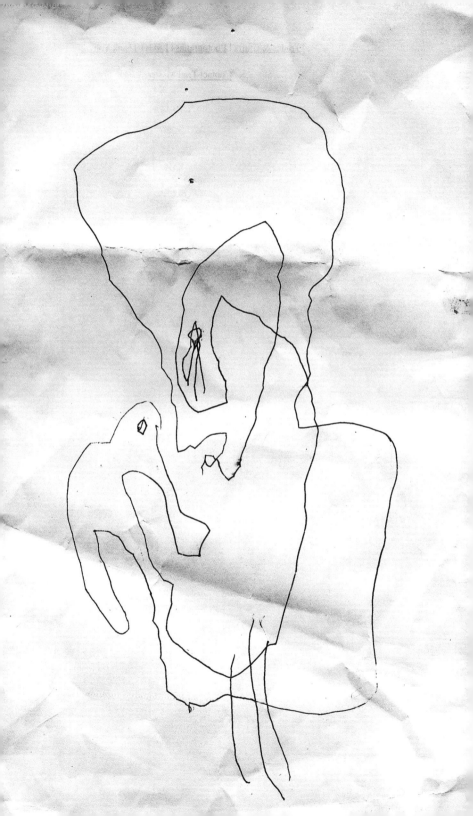

Scene One

The scene is a bridge and a woman sits beneath it
Her head is bent the purse between her knees
Is empty
Her green blouse is covered with pins
That glitter in the sunlight like so many icicles
Around her are arranged the few items that
Describe a life
An open knife a closed tin
A hairbrush
So profoundly neat in arrangement
Her house becomes inviolable
Beyond speculation
An interior

Scene Two

Proust wakes
His pillow
A daguerreotype of his thoughts
I am afraid that I am not great
Harmony of colours in the light
Capitalism will die before the love market
Baudelaire and Hamlet
O the blankets itch
Collection of buttons in a jar
Must remember
To be loved
A craving for eggs
Antimony of sentiments
Biological melody

Scene Three

Mirrors amplify the space and make
It hard to orient oneself
Fractured limbs begin to ache
This space in the bosom of nothingness
Faces ripple turning
Kaspar Hauser thinks
How to say it hurts

Scene Four

Another Bohemian whose life has become a problem
Forces a myth on a passerby

Lives honestly or
Recalls love or

Eats what slides from the plate
Establishes a territory of unbelonging

Forgets the name by which she was known
Sees that her features have blurred

When one is sailing she whispers
The night is a glittering envelope
The fish leap out of the water to witness

Scene Five

Beggar dreams a play and I appear as if a puppet
I fall through ice and below in water with the seals

I say you must see me for who I am
I am like you a citizen
Mud on my instrument
Song I have half forgot

Wife do you have an hour left for me
To wash my face and kiss it

Daughter I failed you
Take my garments burn them with my plays

I

I lay in the faithful bed that never knew anyone but you

I imagine myself with a great public

I turn out the light

I discover that this is also personal

I touch, am touched by

I fear for my own mind, not for the seagull or the wild duck

I hit a rock and the wind is knocked out of me

I can't bear that poorhouse!

I sleep with the small print in the white of the page

I am red meat

You and I are under fire

I learn the burning pain

I think I am going to die

I am and I want to know why

I can't blame anyone

I was eighteen before I crossed over to this bank

I want to fight in the open

I want to see how much I can bear

I look at you, I know you're good

I do believe I swear it

Ghost Sonata

We aim for an intimate theatre
Many chambered plays
Where themes have limits and
Calculated effects are swept into alleys
With the old sawdust
No solo numbers for the stars
No cues for applause
Dematerialize the stage
The scale of values suspended in the cloakroom

And *I* the author who loves freedom
Follow a harmony of ideas and a secret sense of style
Until the deaths are real almost musical

I Miss You

Half-awake in sandals
Perfumes fighting in the air
I stumble in your dress

I'm drunk
Impossible to make
My face replace yours

You at the restaurant
Or braiding your hair
Arranging the dishes

My body too small and still too rough

Dear Friend

I cannot write to you
Your letters and your lawyer's letters
Plead to loose the bonds we forged
Say that they were softened metal
More like wax that held
Two sticks together in the water
When we last drove beneath the dome
To a home that held our child
I took the sunset for
Some change of fate

At Liding Bridge we took a walk
Until we reached the cornerstone
You cut me there
You said the servants
Take turns reading to her
She never sleeps in her own bed
My goodwill spilled intestinal
Tangles of despair
No I cannot write to you
Dear Friend

Darling Daughter According to the *I Ching*

The young fox has nearly crossed the stream
Tail immersed while Heaven in its motion
Gives the great man
The idea of strength and so nerves him
A dragon appears in the field
Diffusion of virtue
How she treads on green claws waiting
Vigilant all day
The dragon parts the wheat
Whipped by brassy shafts
The fox hesitates in the water
The great man sets aside his books
Draws on a yellow garment
Hoarfrost rushes every surface
Symbol of great consummation
The dragon rears to show her breasts
Half-woman in the sudden ice
The great man sheds tears of blood
Hot streams that free the fox and let her run
Father, calls the young fox
I will be waiting on the sand
We will feast together
Cleaved into a constellation
Father, Father there will be good fortune —

Instructions to My Child

Be lenient with me

(Tiny white signals too small to be photographed)

I make no music

(Exposed by the wind)

I do not claim to suffer

Just to spur the sorrow

(Blue one I never meant to love)

The birds I have kept hidden in my attic are quiet now

Painting of Sweden

The picture is double-bottomed
With an exotic aspect everyone can see
Stranded ship man in a raincoat crests of waves collapsing
little dog wearing a coat. And an esoteric aspect, which is the
hidden meaning of the image for its maker, monsters and demons
daggers and cemetery stones
A green landscape with red cliffs a yellow sky
And black spruce (meaning Sweden)
My universe in pigments arranged on a palette
Pause over the circles of colour
To watch the stars just pinpricks of light fall
Through holes in the great eggshell of heaven
No gravitational centre between the Earth and sun no
Tedious spheroids at all but a hollow rolling pin
with the polar regions at the Centre. One could sail from the
North to the South Pole directly
The moon a slice of quartz hurled into space

Twelve Syllables in Paris

If we trace his course we can slow him down and say
Beside him lies a maidservant her bleeding tongue
And needlework the house so full of music tight
The curtains move and then the lock must be broken
A man can lose everything and still have his
Mind or else how sorrowful how sad a thing to
Break apart and here beneath the sunflowers I
Feel the fountain water graze my cheeks the balance
Of being here starving in a beautiful place
His and her (my) coffee pot and embroidery
In the arms of his/her in she walks we are two
Together my teeth around the middle biting
Chipping the river chalking the roads and that
Brave bastard writing the social contract as if
Clouds come to tea please, oh please send me some money

Small White Room

Oh I know defenselessness as well first love bad luck
Lost my family melted silver spoons in lead
Who held my tongue that afternoon you told my child about
       her birth
Oskar says to be a man no need to cry
I caress sweet ghosts their fingers in my hands
While words skip over water

Do You Understand

My mother was a maidservant do you understand?
My mother went cold and rotten inside
Not able to say, "I need a rest"
All she saw was space wanting the space to tighten
She never lifted her eyes
One day Hemingway
Will bend a girl over a chair
Remember how sweet the boys can be
Lie down like some crushed pigeon
Say it again my mother was a maidservant
She never went to Spain
She drank she split the blue vein
Bathing only in the poem
Half-human in the stone café

A New Wife

About Harriet, how this evening she came again
And slept upon my arm
And we refrained from violence
Abandoned all the angry words watched them
Float off among the stars
Which only show how great the surrounding darkness

Letter to the Doctor After Suffering from Delusions

Dear Dr. Forssberg,

I am writing to you for medical advice at my new wife's insistence. You know how impossible she can be. My work is not going well, which is what most concerns me. She, however, is concerned because I made the mistake of confessing that everything is beginning to look strange to me again, artificial. I admit that it seems unlikely that the entire hotel has been rebuilt and all the guests cast from actors in the local theatre. But there it is, perhaps I am seeing problems that don't exist to avoid seeing the real problem, which is that my wife has once again been replaced by a double. To give me credit I feel that I am behaving quite calmly, more calmly in fact than is usual for me.

There was a terrible situation at the playhouse recently. It was one of those hot summer nights where the walls sweat and all the actors look like hell. I made the mistake of inviting Ibsen, that pompous masturbator, only to show him how lively the theatre has become in his absence and how dead he is to me. He sat in the front row of an otherwise empty theatre, watching my depressing idiots struggle to remember their lines. I wrapped myself in one of the curtains so that I could peer at him from the side of the stage. The fleas were jumping on and off my skin. Ibsen sat still as a censor letting on nothing of what passed through his narrow gut. I shut my eyes when it became unbearable; I felt I would pass out. And when I opened them again the prick had left! Not even at intermission. And the stupid cow playing Grandmother looked over at me and asked if they need continue!

Writing is so lonely. I have it in my head that if I write notes for my next play with a red goose quill, a truly huge red goose quill, somehow the hotel will start to seem less like a stage set. And the guests, manager, and servants will all seem like ordinary people again and not like ghostly actors, gently rehearsing. So I search the shops around the Stockholm skerries for such a pen. I walk for hours in the afternoons. It's very frustrating. But the bunches of cyclamen are soothing, with their pink, white, purple, crimson flowers and their reflexed petals. Perhaps I will try to write a play about a man who buries his enemies and then continues to visit them because the flowers on their graves heal his smallest wounds.

But, to return to the reason I am being forced to write you, I must admit that the woman I am living with is pleasant most of the time. But she does not always seem quite like Harriet. Not even as much as the others. There are all these little differences that make me think that she is not my wife at all. And the more I question her the more irritable she becomes. For example, I compared a little picture of her from when we first met to a sketch that I made recently. I noted that in the recent sketch the woman looks heavier. Well, I received no end of abuse for pointing out the difference.

It's not that I mind having my wife replaced from time to time, in fact it often renews my enthusiasm. I only wish to have some say in the matter, such as when it would happen. And I wonder if this Harriet is related to the last Harriet in any way. I should like to know if they ever speak together about me and if any one of them likes me better than the others. For my part, the version who cooks ham with honeyed onions is my favourite. That one has a very sweet wet mouth. She only comes around every six months or so but her oral fixation fits very well with some of my own goals. The one I like the least (I have to be careful to mail this letter before the wife reads it) comes around about every three weeks for a few days. That one has a sharp, nasty personality and the slightest turn in the weather can send her into a rage or make her break into tears.

So, Doctor, since I must ask your advice, perhaps you have some insight into the part of my situation that most enthralls me. You see, I have been trying to work out a way to make love to two of them at once. If I could perhaps catch them together at the moment of turnover, when one wife is stepping in for the other, then pretend that I am sleepwalking. "Oh, Harriet," I could say, "are there two of you? Why don't you both come back to bed? What a lovely dream I am having." Doctor, do you think a truly mad man would be so cunning?

If only I could find out from her by what device she duplicates herself then I could make my own doubles and not have to deal with actors anymore. Think of it, a new form of theatre, perfectly inviolable. I could venture into criticism as well and give myself a proper review. I could murder Ibsen and I could defend myself in court to a jury of my true peers and a judge with a decent intellect! I could multiply my skills exponentially. Harriet doesn't realize that she could be my perfect mate if only she would come out in the open with this trick of hers and share it with me.

When the academy asks, "Why use the theatre to create unrelieved depression by showing brutal aspects of human nature in the name of art." When the critics say, "It can all be summed up so easily, O horrible, O horrible, O horrible!"; when the debutantes accuse me while sucking on their pens of portraying erotic passion as an illness (they refuse to listen when I say that my misogyny is poetic, theoretical, I couldn't live without the company of women), when they all pipe up so foolishly, a hundred thousand tiny August S.'s will crawl into their mouths and block their throats until they lie squirming in terror on the ground and admit I am the only one who ever speaks the truth!

At any rate, Doctor, you can see I am still myself at heart. And my plays still stand in contrast to the wildness and the wooliness of my remarks. I don't mind being made to write to you because it means that I do not have to lunch with my mother-in-law. I would be happy to visit you again, and drink a lot of liquor in your lovely drawing room, and talk about my fantasies and future plans. You need never worry that I will be anything less than an utterly social animal. Even when my presence tends to injure my cause I still enjoy a night out. Harriet and I, or should I say, my wives and I, are happy pretending not to know that we plot against each other. I am not a deceived husband. I am that lucky creature who realizes that inside his life a hundred other lives are waiting to be led.

Come and see my new play. I will reserve as many seats as you like. There will be skeletons, and parrots, and a doctor who you may think you resemble. But come on opening night — the theatres close down quickly these days.

Sincerely,

Your *August S.*

Failures

Burning my hands all the distilled wine roses in the Tuileries
paintings by my favourite painters could not repair my skin the
church that building I cursed every day since my mother's death
house of my reprieve paid my medical bills I don't know if I
believe in God Man is so unpredictable the bishop approved a
gift although I could not turn the brass to gold I felt the
bioelectric current running through my arms one only works
thinking that something may come of it but the alchemists our
recipes must be metaphors I think that's why they saved me Gold
is the sun Silver is the waxing moon Mercury the waning moon
Copper is Venus Lead is Saturn Iron is Mars Tin is Hermes
Electrum is Zeus the sun with a single ray filings and leaf solder
of silver Aphrodite running iron after the Babylonian war
lead for grief and dismemberment
the slowest moving planets memory
loss at the lofty gates

"Resist this war of nerves. Resist."

Excerpts from *Gold as a Remedy in Disease*

A small dog was made to swallow ten grains of the perchloride of gold . . . he vomited three times in the space of the first six minutes . . . he threw up a great deal of frothy saliva . . . Two days afterwards his appetite was good . . . On the fourth day he began to refuse food; he grew lean, and was very much depressed. He died in the night of the seventh day. (The temperature of the air was at three or four below zero, and he remained almost constantly out of doors.) . . . These experiments teach me too little.

27   I have observed slight salivation and great tenderness
        of the gums a pustular eruption results from the
        Tinctura Auri Mur 3x, in drop doses four times a day
        for post-gonorrheal induration of left testis.
        Obviously, not mine.

28   Gold soluble in the juices of the stomach.

29   In England they use mercury as much as we use
        chocolate in France.

30   Very wakeful; well up to work; great mental activity;
        breasts a little hard.

31   Last night erotic dreams; early in the morning in bed
        weary pain in the right tarsal bones of skull soon
        passing off.

1   Astringent metallic taste in mouth; tongue slightly
        coated with brownish fur.
        Make a note to brush teeth twice after drinking.

3   Feel fagged. Told that I look pale and worn.

7   The dead. Dreaming the dead ... for many days
        dreams of the dead and dead bodies ... dreaming I'm
        dead dreaming ...

13   Having thus taken one grain and six-tenths of
        metallic gold I am thoroughly satisfied that it can
        make *me* ill.

Titles

*Titles: Gold in the Sphere of the Mind / Gold in the Treatment of
Pining Boys (The Despised ones at Cricket) / Gold in its effects on the
Uterus and Ovaries / Gold as an Antidote to the Ill-Effects of Mercury
/ Gold Cousin-German to Mercury / Gold as a Remedy for Disease*

I left the walnut seven days before I slid
The heart-shaped embryo so like a tiny human brain
Onto the plate of the microscope
My eye on glass I perceived two
Tiny alabaster hands clasped in prayer.
Ten fingers what emotions
I cried alone with my microscope

My Genius Is Better Than Your Genius

The fall the feeling the hand raised high the blows fell thick the
friend is wounded the proofs discovered the pamphlets printed
the bill presented the microscope pawned the pianos played the
plot thickened the ladies rejected the night raged the nail
hammered the plaster fell the lodger claimed the poltergeists
came the Baptist entered the starveling dreamt the mosquito bit
the flush-ball opened the windows stretched the water closets
seethed the author lunched the chamber pot said
He came to kill me

Bone Ash Lead Melted on a Bed

calcium phosphate did take on a glaze of perfect anger
I was never haunted by visions I WAS NEVER HAUNTED BY
VISIONS
        but real objects did appear endowed with human shapes
Zeus in the half-shadow of my bed
a school of drawing on my pillow   one night coming home
            from an orgy
        I saw the devil and asked a sculptor if that was abnormal
        he said he saw the Virgin sketched with charcoal in the
floating weeds of Lac des Suisses
her front teeth were missing and she handed me a guitar

Flowers warn me of some danger   poison in the star-filled
            night
        I hear my enemy in the room above   a stream of gas
comes through the wall   clicking of the case   currents of pain

               issue from

                        the dark machine

The Condemned Man's Toilette

I buy bread and cherries for my old friend, Martin.
I see a bear who knows me.
I leave this earthly paradise.
I catch the scent of sea lions.
I sniff the filth of birds and snakes and all of it is made by God.
I slip into the bath made vacant by a Swedish girl.
I shave and slap on old cologne.
I take up my Bible.
I lower the curtains over the glazed door to my room.
I sip champagne. I turn off my lamp. I lie on my deathbed.
I wait and I wait.
I drag an armchair into the courtyard.
Beneath the starry vault I consider my errors.
I hear a little cough.
Death grabs for my heart.
I make a very comical escape.

Sonnet of Chapters

Accidents from Overdoses of Gold
First Involuntary Proving
Second Involuntary Proving
Third Involuntary Proving
Fourth Involuntary Proving
Fifth Involuntary Proving
Sixth Involuntary Proving
Seventh Involuntary Proving
Eighth Involuntary Proving
Ninth Involuntary Proving
Tenth Involuntary Proving
Eleventh Involuntary Proving
Twelfth Involuntary Proving
(and so on)

The purpose of this book is to give a short and clear account of the alchemists . . . [The purpose of this book is not to resurrect my mother] where so much is in doubt . . . The purpose of this book . . . I have to be content . . . [with a] history of error . . . John Donne . . . glorifies his pregnant pot . . . why not me . . . If by the way . . . someone . . . would just understand . . . that . . . the history of ideas is beginning . . . and it is hoped that this book will be . . . small [but I will survive].

Mirror Painting

She (me) breathes into the picture
The centre falls away
Falls into her (his) airy thoughts
Then below where rashes rise
I (who) work to hold the silence
Sustain the sense of falling
Out of one self into
That moat around the mountain
Drowning in the margin
Flushed natural skin
Her (your) face was the
Last thing ever seen

True Again

Is it true again?
There is another afternoon with you in the world
Mother and daughter in muslin gowns

I saw you hide behind the door
I hid under the kitchen table

There were oranges for all the guests
Humming in a wooden bowl

My Funeral

Stranger says are we to have carriages? Law says yes, covered
carriages to carry us by the sea. Stranger says I thought at first
that you said covered marriages. They both turn pale because
well the fire was an accident. Law says and now you are happy.
Stranger says I am sad to be so happy. Law says now you must be
brave for I am taking you to the worst part of your life. But
Stranger says I have been there before I am looking forward to
seeing my mother again.

Acknowledgements

Invaluable support was given to this book by the Canada Council, the Ontario Arts Council, the Toronto Arts Council, the Alberta Foundation for the Arts and the Markin-Flanagan Distinguished Writers Program.

Certain of these poems have appeared in *The Walrus, filling Station, Open Letter*, above/ground press, and *RE-GENERATIONS: Canadian Women Poets in Conversation*.

Guillaume Appollinaire's "The Gypsy" is the French text for Siri's poem trans-elated from French.

The poem "I" is composed of lines from other poems that begin with the word I. The writers of these poems include Erin Mouré, Fred Wah, Daphne Marlatt, Dionne Brand, Di Brandt, and August Strindberg.

"Christmas Poem by My Mother" is for Lynn Donohue.

"The Playwright Interviews Herself to Stave off Loneliness" is for Tom Wayman.

"For You" is for Lilah Lily May Hicks

"Happy Animal" is for Paige Gwyneth Hicks.

"Darling Siri Writes a Christmas Poem by Pretending to Read French" is for Susan Swan and Patrick Crean.

"*M*" is for Mali Lol and Lesje Serengeti.

The first fetish: "Baby Dragon" is by Casey Leipert, age 2. The second fetish: "Mummy and Baby when Baby Was a Llama" is by Imogen Leipert, age 3.

"Self-portrait" is a photograph of a line drawing by the author of a very young August Strindberg with a bandage on his ear.

This book has washed up after a decade of seachanges. My Strindberg has crossed provinces with me and become a dear companion. I have to acknowledge that my first effort was to take the mickey out of a modern master I thought was a monster. Now, my first thanks must go to that playwright who was so complicated, so full of love and hate and doubt and vanity, genius and idiocy, violence, madness, tenderness, humiliation that s/he became the perfect mirror for humanity.

I thank the team at ECW for great work. I thank as well my editor, Michael Holmes, for his lasting friendship and his insightful comments. I thank Tom Wayman who read several versions of this manuscript and offered sound advice on individual poems as well as support of the project as a whole. I thank Emily Schultz for her fine eye and ear. I thank my generous readers, Sonnet L'Abbé, Marg, Jonathan Ball, Jordan Kujawa Scott, Michelle Berry, and Jeremy Leipert.

I thank the salonistas (loosely described): Priscila Uppal, Karen Connelly, Diana Fitzgerald Bryden, Ann Shin, Ailsa Kay, Julia Creet, Susan Swan, and Kerri Huffman.

Friends in and out of poetry lent me much: Nikki Sheppy, Jonathan Bennett, Wendy Morgan, Cathy Ostlere, derek beaulieu, ryan fitzpatrick, Erin Mouré, Natalie Zina Walschots, Crystal Mimura, Tasha Hubbard, Ann and Rowland Smith, Tara and Neil Scott, Ed

Schmutz, Chris Blais, Di Bos, Harry Vandervlist, Jason Christie, and Andrea Ryer.

I thank my family: Patricia and Russell Caple, Suzanne Caple-Hicks, Marc Hicks, (my beloved nieces) Paige and Lilah Hicks, my aunts Pip and Joyce, my cousins Sharon, Heather, Dan, and Carly, and my grandmothers Gwyneth and Eileen, my ideal in-laws Janet and Gerry, Jhennia and Jonathan and Becki Leipert, Colin Martin and the entire Leipert/Martin clan. As always I thank Nick Kazamia for being my twin.

Last and most I thank the home team, my husband, Jeremy, for rescuing me and restoring my joy, and our children, Imogen and Cassius, for bringing out the stupid tiger hidden in my heart (oh and little Lolo most patient of dogs).

However sentimental it may be I thank you all profusely because I recognize that I am so lucky to have you.